THE WEST HIGHLAND WAY

THE WEST HIGHLAND WAY

Ronald Turnbull

Frances Lincoln Limited
4 Torriano Mews
Torriano Avenue
London NW5 2RZ
www.franceslincoln.com

The West Highland Way
Text and photographs copyright © Ronald Turnbull 2010
First Frances Lincoln edition: 2010

ISBN: 978-0-7112-3033-0

Printed and bound in China

9 8 7 6 5 4 3 2 1

HALF TITLE The West Highland Way runs (left to right, for
northbound walkers) along the edge of Rannoch Moor at the
foot of the Black Mount. It passes two plantations that can be
seen in the middle distance of this picture, which was taken
right across the moor from the summit of Beinn Achaladair.

TITLE PAGE Loch Lomond at dusk from Duncryne.

RIGHT Beinglas Falls stand above the West Highland Way and
the Inverarnan Inn, which has been in use since it was a cattle-
drover's stance at the start of the eighteenth century. The falls
are reached by a steep path from Beinglas camp site.

CONTENTS

INTRODUCTION

It's just after sunrise, on a warm March morning on Cnap Mor. The heather is dry enough to lie back on; the view is the length of Loch Lomond. Sunlight glitters along twelve miles of shaggy promontories and islands. Far down at the end, Ben Lomond itself rises from cloud like a tousled head from morning bed-sheets. On my right, at the loch head, low sunbeams wash the chalet shanty-town of Ardlui. The same early light glows golden on the slopes of Beinn a' Choin, making them look slightly like Charlize Theron with no clothes on as she was that month, while advertising Dior perfumes.

After two days on the trail, it's luxury just to lie here in the heather, with the memory of last autumn's heather-blossom even more subtle than Dior perfume. As an excuse for being stationary, a half-hour spent here might bring sunlight onto the slopes of Ben Vorlich for a further photo. At half past seven comes the first stirring of the new day: a creaking noise, and soft honking up in the sky. I open my eyes to a skein of eight swans, outlined against the snows of Ben Vorlich. A ninth swan is calling to them from the loch, 500 feet below. But the eight fliers spiral higher; they're heading northwards up Glen Falloch.

It's time I was heading that way myself. On the back of the hill I disturb some wild goats, chocolate brown amidst the beige and ochre of the sunlit, but still winter-coloured, moorland. The tall rushes around the Dubh Lochan are palest yellow, with not a hint of green; and Beinglas campsite is tentless and empty.

Two days north of Loch Lomond, there comes something quite different.

At the back of Tyndrum, the Way rises to a U-shaped gap between the hills. As the Way rises, so alongside it does the West Highland Railway, the main A82 road, and a set of electricity pylons. Up in the hill gap the cloud is

Creise and Rannoch Moor from Kings House.

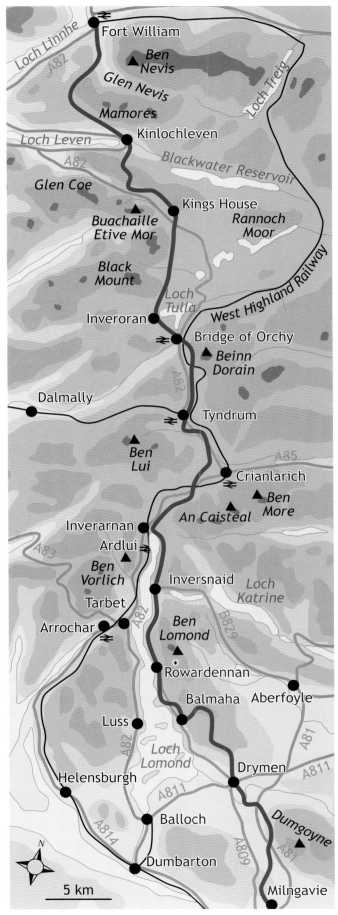

low. It's almost low enough to conceal the slopes of grassy peat above on the right, the grim grey spruce trees on the opposite side. However it is not low enough to conceal the electricity pylons, or the main A82, where lorries head north in a swish of rainwater, and the snarl of motorbikes echoes off the hills.

Throughout the night, it has been raining. Two miles back, the stream at the back of Tyndrum was an ankle-deep splashy paddle; now, every footfall is a gentle squelch. Worse, there's a blister forming down there. Stopping and sorting it out will involve new movements, bringing new bits of the body in contact with wet clothing. Best just to plod on over the stones. It's quite gradual, the way the rain penetrates first the sleeves, then the supposedly waterproof trousers, and finally the chest and back.

At twenty minutes past nine comes a sudden clatter along the track. The morning train is heading south from Fort William. The dry people behind its windows are just 20 yards below. Even so, they are a world away. They are wearing clean shirts, and perhaps a light woolly cardigan, more for decorative effect than warmth. Their bodies are clean, their feet are clean, they do not have any greasy itching in their hair. They are wearing clean socks. They are listening to music, or maybe they are reading a magazine inside which the golden body of Charlize Theron is advertising some scent. In a few minutes, someone's going to come down the train with some hot coffee. The windows are steamed up, luckily, so the train passengers can't see me out here standing on my sore feet, in the rain.

There are seven miles of this stony track: plenty of time for the rain to penetrate the chest and trickle in at the elbows.

Walkers on the Way

The West Highland Way was thought out in the 1960s, and opened in 1980 by William Mungo Murray, 8th Earl of Mansfield and Mansfield, then Minister of State in the Scottish Office. But in a sense it has always been here. Between the Lowlands and Lochaber have travelled clansmen and cattle thieves; redcoats, drovers, saints and Sir Walter Scott.

It's a journey of glens and low passes, under the crags and high grassy sides of seven of Scotland's hill ranges: from the Arrochar Alps of Loch Lomond to the Black Mount of Argyll, the Mamores and big Ben Nevis. Geologically, it's an outing from the Old Red Sandstone hills of the so-called Lowland Valley, through the immeasurably older grey schists of the Southern Highlands, to the great volcanic cauldron of Glen Coe. And as it unfolds under the foot, it's 95 miles of heather and oakwood, of lochside and riverside and old railway line – but also the whole life and history of Celtic Scotland.

ABOVE Loch Tulla from Beinn Achaladair.

RIGHT Abandoned shielings – summer pastures – in the Lairig Mor between Kinlochleven and Fort William.

First inhabitants of the land were the mythic Fingalians, led by Fingal himself. Larger than life – in the literal as well as the metaphorical sense – they hunted the deer with their equally oversized dogs, and used their spear-shafts to pole-vault across the narrow sea lochs of Argyll. They fought great battles among themselves and against invading human beings out of Norway, and had commerce with the fairy folk. Along the West Highland Way no trace of them remains; but Deirdre (of the Sorrows) and her first lover Naisi spent happy months with their deer hounds around Buachaille Etive Mor, before her tragic fate fell upon her. And a short diversion into Glen Coe will show the cave, high among the crags of Bidean nam Bian, named in legend as the home of the Fingalian bard Ossian.

The starting point for the merely human history of the Highlands is almost as mythical: the pre-feudal clan society remembered in songs and stories, but only recorded in writing as it came to its end, and then mostly by the pens of its enemies.

In each glen, the clan lived under its chieftain as an extended family. The traditional 'black house' was of unmortared stone, thatched with heather, and with an earth floor. Peat smoke filled the house before trickling out of the doorways and unglazed windows. Golden sunbeams cut through the brown peat-gloom, which scented the rooms like the wild bog outside while also being an effective deterrent against midges. Their music was the clan piper, and entertainment was the bard at the fireside, with tales of past warfare, the fairies, and the Fingalians.

Oats and kale were raised in the more fertile corners of the valley floor, and there would be fish from the lochs and rivers. But the mainstay of the clan was its cattle: the small, nimble black beasts of the glens. Every summer, to protect the crops, the cattle would be moved up into the high corries. There the young people would live alongside them in temporary huts or shielings, making cheese – and also presumably music and love – in the shelter of the great crags.

And if cattle were the mainstay of clan life, the thieving of cattle was their main economic activity. Bill Murray in his biography of Rob Roy describes cattle-reiving as 'a robust form of social security', re-dressing the balance when famine struck one part of the Highlands while another was in relative plenty.

In the course of cattle raids in particular, the clansmen made journeys from one side of Scotland to the other, in all weathers, with no shelter apart from their close-woven woollen plaids. For the returning raiders of Lochaber or Argyll, Rannoch Moor was a place of safety; no pursuit would follow into the secret pathways amongst its bogs and lochans. In 1686, the Glencoe MacDonalds came home from the battle of Killiecrankie by way of Glen Lyon. There they raided and stole

from the Campbells to the value of £8,000 Scots before heading north by Loch Tulla and the Moor of Rannoch.

Six years later, that same Campbell of Glenlyon came north to Glen Coe with orders for the massacre in his saddlebag. The MacDonalds of Glen Coe, the most successful reivers of them all, had been raiding their neighbours right into the century of the coffee-house and the powdered wig, and were to pay a deadly price for their outmoded traditional lifestyle.

There are, traditionally, three plagues of Argyll: the bracken, the midges – and the Campbells. Clan Campbell, under its chieftain the Duke of Argyll, caught on to the possibilities in the new feudal system and starte d a 200-year campaign to take over the whole of the southern Highlands. Among their principal victims were MacDonalds of Glencoe and the Hebrides, and the Macgregors of Lomondside and the Trossachs.

Their takeover techniques were not genteel. In 1499 they kidnapped the four-year-old heiress of Cawdor, kept her captive until she reached fifteen, then forcibly married her to a Campbell younger son. An heiress widow was seized and raped, while bagpipes played to cover her screams.

Their later technique was more sophisticated, but just as effective. A feud between Clan Gregor and the Colquhouns of Loch Lomondside started with the unauthorised slaughter of a black-tailed sheep. Campbell of Argyll offered support to the Macgregors, encouraging them to kill two or three hundred of the Colquhouns. At this point the Campbell rode over to Edinburgh and offered to sort out the problem. Thus in 1603 the whole of Clan Gregor was declared outlaw and the use even of its surname was banned. This stayed on the statute book for almost 200 years, being reactivated when convenient to the Campbells.

And so we see Rob Roy Macgregor, heroically applying the claymore and the cattle raid against the forward-looking Campbells, with their mortgage foreclosure and their writ from the Privy Council. Rob Roy lived at Craigrostan, on Loch Lomondside, near the present-day Rowchoish bothy. His Lowland neighbour and enemy the Duke of Montrose had his headquarters at Mugdock Castle, at the southern end of the West Highland Way. So walkers on this footpath know exactly how troublesome it was for Montrose's reprisal raid, in September of 1716, as it passed up Loch Lomond side to a dawn rendezvous at Inversnaid and an attack on Craigrostan.

The party of 250 soldiers set out at 8pm from Buchanan House (now the clubhouse of one of Drymen's two golf courses). They had 16 miles to cover, most of them in the dark. Soon after they started, the skies opened; it rained all night, as they struggled along Loch Lomond. Leaf mould on the rocks is slippery at the best of times, and now every burn was in spate. They arrived long after daybreak and with Rob Roy well aware of their presence. However, their force was too large to be attacked, and Rob could only watch from the crags as the soldiers, for the second time in six months, burnt down his house.

As what we today call 'civilisation' penetrated the Highlands, the chieftains started to take their rents not in military service but in kind, or even in cash. The

LEFT Across Loch Lomond to the tumble of boulders containing Rob Roy's Cave.

ABOVE Rob Roy's Cave, Loch Lomond. During the years of feud with Montrose, Rob Roy was harried about the countryside, seldom spending a single night under his own roof. He was also inconvenienced by amateur bounty-hunters. He was three times captured, and three times escaped; the most famous escape, during a crossing of the River Forth near Aberfoyle, formed an incident in Walter Scott's novel *Rob Roy* and also in the 1995 film starring Liam Neeson. During this time, it is quite possible that he may have made use of the 'Rob Roy' cave below the West Highland Way just north of Inversnaid. On the other hand, its location, right on the shoreline, was highly convenient for boatmen bringing tourists from the carriage road on the opposite shore. Among those so brought were the Wordsworths and Coleridge in their tour of 1803, and Sir Walter Scott.

The 'cave' is actually a hollow within a tumble of boulders cracked off by frost from the crags just above. It's a popular night spot nowadays for the shaggy brown billygoats. While it does appear to be dry, it is not by modern standards particularly comfortable, and any human planning refuge there today is advised to use the inflatable sort of sleeping mat.

source of cash was the clansmen's black cattle: beef to feed the growing cities of the industrial revolution, as well as England's army adventuring into France and Holland in various wars.

And so the reiver or cattle thief became a drover – gathering black cattle every autumn and driving them southwards, 12 miles a day, to the Lowland markets of Falkirk and Crieff. It was a trade that combined banditry and banking. During the drove itself, the drover had to defend the herd with sword and musket, living wild and reading the country. At the same time he was holding much of the wealth of his township or clan. At the drove's end, he negotiated the sale, and remitted to the owners at home whatever purchase price had been agreed. It was a trade where trust and reputation were as important as hillcraft and skill with the sword. The old thieves' roads by Rannoch and southwards to Loch Lomond formed a natural line

ABOVE Major Caulfeild's military road runs towards Buachaille Etive Mor (centre) before turning off to the right up the Devil's Staircase. On the left is the northern end of the Black Mount, with snowy Meall a' Bhuiridh and steep-ended Creise.

RIGHT Caulfeild's bridge carries the West Highland Way across River Orchy.

for the cattle drovers on their way towards Falkirk, and sometimes onwards across the hills to the south of England. Imagine them asleep in the heather at Inveroran with their plaids lapped over their heads; both Inveroran (established 1708) and Inverarnan (1705) were overnight stances for the herds heading south.

After the failure of the 1715 rebellion, General Wade advised King George that nobody would control the Highlands who couldn't move freely across them, and suggested the building of a road system. And King George said: 'Okay, you do it then,' and made him Commander in Chief of His Majesty's forces, castles, forts and barracks in North Britain. The first road was over in the east, along the line of today's A9. It was built by 300 men (who earned sixpence a day extra) at a rate of about 10 miles a month. It was Wade's even more efficient successor, Major William Caulfeild, who from 1740 built the stony roads from Loch Lomond across Rannoch Moor, over the Devil's Staircase to Kinlochleven, and onwards to the new fort at Fort William. Caulfeild's roads remain as the tracks used by almost half of the West Highland Way – although the stretch across Rannoch Moor uses the more recent road built by Thomas Telford in the 1820s.

And as England's Lake District became just too pretty and popular even for the Romantic poets, along General Caulfeild's new military road the bravest of the landscape appreciators headed to the Trossachs, Loch Lomond and beyond.

Poets William Wordsworth and Samuel Taylor Coleridge, in ill health and ill temper, came up Loch Lomond towards Fort William in August of 1803. The two great poets rode sideways, facing the scenery, their backs to one another, in an uncomfortable Irish jaunting carriage. Like some of the walkers of today, STC abandoned the journey half way along Loch Lomond. Unlike them, he went and walked what is now the Great Glen Way instead. This poet is also one of the finest writers there has been on British hillwalking, so I make no apology for inviting him to caption several of the photos in this book. A few years later, Sir Walter Scott 'invented' the Trossachs, along with a fictional character he called Rob Roy.

During the two and a half centuries to today, the genuine Highlanders have been gradually displaced. The reprisals and repression after the battle of Culloden were followed by the Highland Clearances as people made way for sheep. Later came deer-stalking estates, and finally the plantations of Sitka spruce. But the scenery-seeking travellers up Loch Lomondside have only increased – in carriages and lake steamers, on the West Highland Railway, on Glen Coe's new road of the 1930s, and finally as we started, on foot up the old raiding route, the drovers' trod, the stony road of General Caulfeild.

Walkers and Wildlife

Along the way we'll meet the wild goats above Loch Lomond and the red deer of Rannoch; we might spot the golden eagle, or the little grassy nest of the meadow pipit. We'll enjoy the purple orchids of the springtime oakwoods, or the wild heather and golden birks (birch trees) of autumn. Like dead Greeks in the afterworld, we'll walk through fields of yellow asphodel; on Conic Hill we'll sun ourselves on a 400-million-year-old shingle beach. We'll thrill to the Gaelic verses of Duncan Ban Macintyre: 554 lines about a single hill, Beinn Dorain. Our wet and possibly blistered feet will follow the footprints of Rob Roy Macgregor, and tread in the cowpats of a successful raid returning to Glen Coe. We'll discover why Kinlochleven, which isn't even on the main bus route, is just ideal for an aluminium smelting works; and find out how the rail line across Rannoch can be uphill in both directions.

The Scottish Highlands, the closest there is to a UK wilderness, are busy with exciting wildlife. But wilderness by its very definition means places where we people don't go. Along the West Highland Way you are unlikely to spot the wild cat or the pine marten – which is one reason why I haven't filled this section with photos of them. The other reason is that I haven't spotted them myself to take their pictures.

But the red deer of the Highlands are too big to hide behind a bog myrtle. If you're the first along the morning path, or the last in the evening, you are likely to see some deer. In spring before the mountain

TOP LEFT Feral goats above Loch Lomond.

TOP RIGHT Wayside flowers: the bog asphodel, bright among black peat, flowers in July alongside the soggier parts of the path.

LEFT Wild orchid in the oakwoods of Loch Lomond.

ABOVE Perhaps the commonest of the moorland birds, the small brown meadow pipit can be recognised by two flashes of white in the tail as she flies away from you. Between May and July she may fly out from a metre away, and then a quick search could discover her four or five eggs in a pocket-like hollow in the grass. However, this will be at least a dozen steps away from the busy footpath.

Red deer stag on Rannoch Moor.

In late March, whooper swans fly north above Loch Lomond.

ABOVE Small, bright wildflowers of the heather moorland, at their best in June and July just before the heather: blue milkwort and yellow tormentil.

RIGHT Telford's road crosses Rannoch Moor, Britain's biggest and bleakest piece of peat.

grasses grow, they throng the roadside at Inveroran and Kings House. In high summer they head uphill – they don't like midges any more than we do. In autumn, in the great corries of Glen Coe, you'll hear the bellowing of the sex-crazed stag.

Many naturalists believe that Scotland's wild goats are descendants of ones abandoned at the time of the Highland Clearances, when whole villages were forcibly evicted during the eighteenth and nineteenth centuries. Some recent genetic research suggests they may, however, go back to the Iron Age. Goats are uniquely good at getting out of fields, and my own belief is that for as long as people have been farming with goats, goats have been escaping into the wild. The ancestors of the ones along Loch Lomond will surely include animals that jumped free at the burning by Montrose of Rob Roy's house at Craigrostan.

After the semi-natural oakwoods of Loch Lomond (where the RSPB claims 200 species of birds in its Inversnaid Reserve), the way emerges among the green mountains of Straths Fillan and Orchy. Small but brilliant wildflowers sparkle in the grassland, between a few remnants of ancient Scots pine.

But the illusion that the countryside is a place of greenery is shattered as you reach Rannoch Moor. Rannoch is black peat, grey granite, and the small grey-brown shrub which makes the ecosystem that's unique, almost, to the UK. The dingy twigs of the heather are touched with gold as the sun rises across the moorland, and its brown glows like toffee as the sun goes down behind the Black Mount. In late August, it goes purple all over, and the peat-smell is touched with honey. In between times, it's simply bleak.

The West Highland Way doesn't just work for walkers. In late March, whooper swans use its valley line as the start of their one-day migration to Iceland. March also brings the strange cries of whaups (curlews), peewits (lapwings) and sea pies (oystercatchers). Later in spring you may hear the mewing cry of the buzzard high overhead. By the middle of summer there may be a whole family of them, half a dozen at once wheeling in the air current above a wind-blown hill slope. Disappointingly, most of the 'eagles' you see will in fact be buzzards. Golden eagles are here, above Glen Coe and Ben Nevis, but mostly around the less busy back sides of the mountains.

The Stones that Make the Road

The clansmen and cattle thieves are gone, the ruins of their low smoky huts and shielings almost invisible now under the spruce plantations of civilisation. The wildlife is present, even if it tends to go away as the day's first walkers disturb the trail. The rocks remain – at least on our petty timescale of years and centuries. The West Highland Way makes a six-day introduction to the last 800 million years.

Not all of us are interested in geology, so let's compress those 800 million years into a couple of paragraphs. Take a scrap of continent that's already ancient, having knocked around the planet for half a billion years or so. That scrap, now called the Scottish Highlands, is made of rocks buried, then unearthed, then crushed, folded, reburied and again unearthed. So mangled are they that what they were to start with scarcely matters any more. They are grey and stripy, tough and rugged: and we call them schist.

The schist was in for a shock. The future Scotland, surging across the planet at the front edge of a continental plate retrospectively named as Laurentia, crashes into England during the period called the Silurian, 450 million years ago. The junction line follows, roughly, the present English border. But it was not a head-on collision: Scotland arrived slantwise, and parts of it broke and slid sideways. One such break is now called the Highland Boundary Fault: the land to its north, now the Highlands, slid westwards across the top of the Lowlands.

By the time the two continents finally shuddered to a halt, a line of upraised mountains as high as today's Alps ran all along the junction. During the next age, which is the Devonian, those mountains started to wear away. This was all happening just south of the Equator, in the desert-climate latitudes corresponding with Namibia and Australia. Accordingly, the mountains were decomposing in flash floods and desert wadis, and forming red desert sands. The rocks that resulted are now called the Old Red Sandstone.

The combined England–Scotland drifted northwards. Soon (well, in 100 million years) it crossed the Equator. Tropical fern forests

grow up, and then fell down into swamps to form coal; which is why this period is called the Carboniferous. But in central Scotland, the Carboniferous is distinguished also as a time of stretch. The reason our continent was drifting north was that its far-away front edge was being dragged down into the earth's interior, in what's called a 'subduction zone'. Scotland was being tugged apart; and where should it break but along that existing fault line, the Highland Boundary? Another break was at the Southern Upland Fault, 50 miles to the south, and the land between these two sank to form a rift valley.

The descending of the rift valley has brought Old Red Sandstones, and the soft Carboniferous rocks on top of them, downwards by several kilometres. So now they lie level with the grim schists to the north. The walk starts over those soft sandstones and black lavas of the Scottish Lowlands. You won't see much of them, as they're mostly buried under earth and wild flowers. But what created the scenery of Strath Blane was the earth-stretching associated with that rift valley. Lava squeezed upwards through cracks in the continental crust, forming volcanoes here, 250 million years ago, rather as it is doing along the African Rift Valley just now. The Campsie Fells are Scotland's Kilimanjaro.

At Conic Hill, the West Highland Way arrives at the edge of the Highlands. Here the walker steps across onto the harsh and ancient continental crust which forms the heart of Scotland. For the next three days you can relax – geologically speaking, at least. The path lets you really get to know the Dalradian schist, the default rock of the Scottish Highlands.

Alpine lady's mantle in a crack of the stripy grey schist that, once across the Highland Line at Balmaha, is the typical country rock of the West Highland Way.

And then, just as you're getting the measure of this schist stuff, up through the earth come bursting the interesting exceptions. As the continents of England and Scotland collided, the descending ocean crust of the subduction zone created friction. Friction creates heat. A huge blob of magma melted its way up into the bottom of the schist, then cooled and crystallised slowly into granite. That granite is pale and speckled, and now shows as the rocks of Rannoch Moor, and the rounded stones of Telford's road.

Just as you're getting to know the granite, suddenly the path stones turn greyish-orange. You've reached the volcanic intrusions of Glen Coe. This is magma that didn't stop and solidify, but melted its way right up to the surface. There it spewed out as rhyolite lava, and fell from the sky as volcanic ash.

All around this confusing stuff, the surrounding schist is as it had been all the way northwards from Lomond to Rannoch. But around Kinlochleven, even the schist is different. When the original rock (before all that metamorphic mangling) happens to have been a really pure, sandy sandstone, then the final result (again after all the metamorphic mangling) will be, not schist, but quartzite. Quartzite is off-white, shiny and slippery, and shows on small crags and path stones where the path leaves Kinlochleven.

The three days northwards from Loch Lomond gave you schist all the same. Ben Nevis, when you eventually get there, gives four sorts of stones in a few metres of path. There's grey schist, but also a strange sort of schist interleaved with limestone. There's quartzite. But Ben Nevis itself is a big vertical cylinder of red granite, with a core of dark grey andesite lava.

So in geological terms, the West Highland Way is a patient teacher. First it shows the stones one at a time; then finally all at once to see if you've learnt which is which. And we note that, while many people

Devonian period, about 400 million years ago
The arrival of England-Wales creates new mountains at the continent edge of Laurentia – the land that will be Scotland. Ocean-floor sediments are raised to form rocks that will some day be the Southern Uplands; even more folding and mangling is administered to the continental schists that will eventually form the Highlands. Sand and rubble eroding out of the new mountains form red desert sandstones. Friction heat deep underground melts magma into rising blobs of granite.

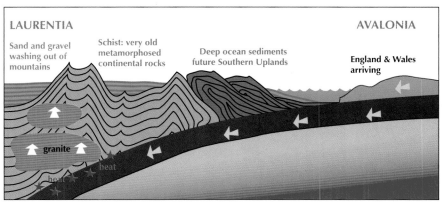

Carboniferous Period, about 250 million years ago.
Scotland is being stretched. Rock is not rubber, and something has to give. Between two old faultlines, the Scottish Lowlands sink into the gap, allowing the Highlands and the Southern Uplands to move a mile or two further apart. Where the crust cracks, basalt lava oozes up to form volcanoes, lavafields and underground sills.

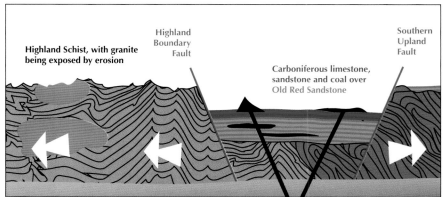

aren't interested in rocks and geology, the present author is – so apologies for the multiplication of the 'couple of paragraphs' promised four pages back.

Lomond to Lochaber

You may walk it on your feet. So did MacIain of Glencoe through the bitter last days of 1691, only to be turned aside at Fort William. So did the unnamed navvies of the Blackwater Dam, who died in the snowdrifts of the Devil's Staircase on their way back from a Saturday night at the Kings House. You can travel on wheels – like William Wordsworth and Sam Coleridge, along with Wordsworth's sister Dorothy, in that uncomfortable little cart in 1803.

You may travel in the spirit, like the condemned soldier from the 1715 Rising who wrote of the bonnie banks of Loch Lomond.

This is Highland Scotland. But even so, not all the stories are sad ones. So let us celebrate MacIain of Glen Coe in younger days, leading his clan through the rainstorm on a raid into the rich Campbell lands of Glen Lyon. Celebrate Scots mountaineer Sandy Cousins, who came down through Fort William to his home in Glasgow at the end of a journey from Cape Wrath over many mountains; and Jez Bragg who in June 2006 ran the entire route in 15 hours and 45 minutes.

But above all, we celebrate 18,000 people who each year, whether on a whim or as a lifetime's ambition, set out from the edge of Glasgow, along the 'steep, steep banks of Loch Lomond' and onwards into Strath Fillan and Rannoch, on their journey of 95 miles of wildness and wet, and the whole life of Highland Scotland.

Loch Lomond sunset from Inveruglas.

STRATH BLANE
Milngavie to Drymen
12½ miles/20 km

Once past the wrought iron arch marking the start of the West Highland Way, the escape from Milngavie is quite sudden. The next 6 miles will cross just two tarred roads. And at the end of them, at an altitude of only 130 metres, there opens up the first of the walk's long views northwards.

Strath Blane ahead is flat, but from it rises one small but sudden hill. Dumgoyne is the first of a sequence of pointy mountains which will waymark the walk north. Far ahead along Strath Blane you could spot the next one: Ben Lomond. That is the Highland Line, where the rugged mountains rise abruptly out of the Scottish Lowlands.

A traveller standing here in 1725 would have looked northwards to the Highlands with more urgent concerns. Behind, the city of Glasgow was thriving on trade in tobacco and grain with the American colonies;

Glasgow's wealthy middle classes were building fine stone houses, and preparing to embark on the Industrial Revolution. Across the Highland Line, life was still more or less in the Iron Age. It was a dangerous place inhabited by wolves and fairies, not to mention Rob Roy Macgregor. A country with its own Gaelic language, an economy of subsistence farming and cattle thievery, and a political system shaped by the sword.

Five miles out from Milngavie comes the first big view: north along Strath Blane to distant Ben Lomond. To right is Dumgoyne.

ABOVE Milngavie, the start of the West Highland Way, has its own pedestrian precinct that's rather less than 95 miles long.

The walk starts beneath birch and oaks of Mugdock Wood. The bushiness of this lichen is an indicator that already we have entered air that is rather less polluted.

LEFT Beard lichen on hawthorn.

RIGHT Oak trunk.

TOP Basalt outcrop in Mugdock wood.

MIDDLE Dark-coloured basalt in Mugdock wood. Its pumice-like appearance is the result of hot volcanic gasses bubbling out of the rock as it cooled.

BELOW Stone sign in the path, Mugdock wood.

LEFT Bluebells in Mugdock wood, at their best in early May. Other advantages of walking so early in the year are fresh birch leaves, cool clear air, lower likelihood of cloud and rain, absence of midges, and a comparative absence of human beings as well.

ABOVE The 'Khyber Pass' path, now the first section of the West Highland Way, was used by hundreds of hikers, hillwalkers, tinkers and tramps as an escape route out of Glasgow during the years between the World Wars. Here at Craigallian Loch, four miles out from Milngavie, was a semi-permanent encampment where, it was said, the camp fire never went out.

RIGHT The track of the West Highland Way passes Craigallian Loch.

ABOVE Carbeth huts. The Carbeth hut community started as an encampment of three ex-servicemen of the First World War. During the Great Depression, with the tacit consent of the estate owner Allan Barnes-Graham and unbothered by such formalities as planning permission, it expanded to several hundred huts with an improvised 'lido' or swimming pool. The occupants, many of them unemployed shipyard workers, walked out from Milngavie Station along the Khyber Pass path that's now the West Highland Way. For many, Carbeth was just a stop-off on the way to the Cobbler and the mountains of the Highlands. The Victorian academics and aristocrats who invented Scottish mountaineering included some pretty tough types. Even so, the post-war influx of hard-drinking, hard-fighting working people led to new standards of seriousness and difficulty on rock and on ice.

BELOW Carbeth Loch.

LEFT Standing stones just east of the way as it approaches Dumgoyach.

ABOVE Both Dumgoyach (left) and Dumgoyne are lava plugs, formed in the vents of volcanoes as they became extinct.

LEFT Wild garlic at the crossing of Blane Water, where the way joins the old Strathblane railway.

ABOVE Coltsfoot flowers in early spring along the Strathblane railway path. Only after the flowers have turned to dandelion-type puffballs and died back do the large, rhubarb-like leaves appear.

LEFT Dumgoyne and its distillery, seen from the path. Dumgoyne is the first of a sequence of pointy mountains that will waymark the walk north: Ben Lomond, Beinn Dorain, and Buachaille Etive Mor of Glen Coe. Surprisingly, of them all Dumgoyne is the sharpest. Slice it off 50m below its top – at the 377m contour – and the area enclosed within that contour is just 4.4 hectares. That happens to be the roofed area of Wembley Stadium, while the height to the summit is the same as Wembley's arch. By this measure, Dumgoyne is rivalled only by certain peaks on Skye, and Sgurr na Ciche in Knoydart, as the UK's pointiest peaks.

BELOW At Gartness, the way crosses this bridge over Endrick Water. Below, the river drops over a resistant bed of the Old Red Sandstone. It continues northwest to become the main feeder of Loch Lomond.

CONIC HILL
Drymen to Milarrochy Bay
8½ miles/14 km

Here the West Highland Way attains its only summit. As well as Conic Hill, this second section has Loch Lomond views, the islands of Inchcailloch, and the ice creams of Balmaha. All these will be totally ignored – by anyone looking at the rocks.

The Highland Boundary is the line of the sinking-down of the north edge of the Lowland Rift Valley. That subsidence brought the softer rocks of Strath Blane level with the ruggedness of the north. Conic Hill is where you stand and see the two sorts of scenery: the schisty scenery to the north, and the softer south already walked over. The hill itself, and the line of islands leading on across Loch Lomond, mark the Highland boundary.

But the Highland Boundary is a faultline that (as Karl Marx said of history) was condemned to repeat itself. Its first time around, 200 million years earlier, it had been part of the shatter zone as Scotland crashed, obliquely, into England. As the collision progressed over tens of millions of years, the part of Scotland that's now the Highlands slid westwards across the part that's now the Lowlands. So having admired the two sorts of scenery, you look down at the ground. And there you see some very odd rocks indeed: first the ones mangled by the moving continental chunks, and then a chip of ocean bed caught up into the gap between.

From Conic Hill, looking out across Loch Lomond, with Balmaha down left. Conic Hill and the line of islands leading from it across the loch are taken as marking the Highland Line. Onwards along that line, Arran can just be dimly seen: the island which is half Lowland, half Highland.

RIGHT Looking across Loch Lomond to Conic Hill at dusk. Picturesque tourism, and its follow-up, fellwalking, started happening quite suddenly in about 1750. As we walk up the West Highland Way gazing at the mountains, it takes a real effort to realise that, just 300 years ago, our activity would have been completely incomprehensible. Unless, of course, we were driving a cow or intending to steal one. Pennant, who toured in 1769, first identified Loch Lomond as the bonniest. By the 1770s, there was already a professional guide to take you up Ben Lomond.

LEFT Loch Lomond at dusk, with Ben Lomond rising to its right. The lights of Gartocharn are down left. This southern part of the loch lies in the Scottish Lowlands: it is wide and shallow, with wooded islands. The northern part of the loch, which in the Highlands, is narrow and deep.

ABOVE Primroses on a damp bank near the foot of Conic Hill.

MIDDLE Conic Hill marks the boundary of the Highlands. Its distinctive rock is a 'puddingstone' or conglomerate: water-worn cobblestones bound in a sandy matrix. The sandy matrix identifies it as part of the Old Red Sandstone, and accordingly, Conic Hill is actually the northern edge of the Scottish Lowlands.

A great mountain range was created when Scotland and England collided, and this conglomerate is stones and gravel washed out by flash floods which came down between those mountains. The cobblestones are whitish quartzite and dark volcanic rocks. The quartzite and volcanic mountains they washed out of have, however, quite literally gone west – the movement along the faultline has carried them into the Atlantic. Northwards, where those mountains once stood tall and proud, there is today grey schist. Note also the cracking of the cobblestones, caused by the shearing forces of the faultline.

BELOW The sculpture outside the National Park Centre at Balmaha reproduces the Highland Boundary. On the left, grey stripy schist of the Highlands: on the right, Old Red Sandstone of the Lowlands. The ORS is 400 million years old but the Highland schist is much, much older.

The West Highland Way drops 300m from Conic Hill to Balmaha on Loch Lomond in less than 2km (1,000ft in just over a mile). Coming, for most walkers, at the end of their second day, the descent with its wooden steps is a harsh one for tired knees. Only the descent from the Devil's Staircase, almost at the end of the way, has a greater overall drop than this one, and that later descent to Kinlochleven is far more gradual.

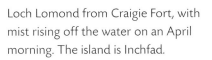
Loch Lomond from Craigie Fort, with mist rising off the water on an April morning. The island is Inchfad.

ABOVE LEFT One mile north of Balmaha (grid ref: 412916), the Way crosses this conglomerate. It's still the Old Red Sandstone conglomerate, but the fragments within it are of grey schist – the rock that today does stand as the mountains to the north. So this one formed later than the conglomerate shown on page 34, at a time when the land to the north had almost finished its sideways slide along the Highland Boundary Fault.

ABOVE Oakwoods in spring, Arrochymore Point.

LEFT This strange stone lies on the loch shore immediately below the path, at the point where it rises slightly around Arrochymore Point (grid ref: 410918). Originally sandstone, it's been crushed and mangled in the movement along the faultline, to the point where its quartz has melted out.

LEFT BELOW Serpentinite rock, originally part of a deep ocean floor, caught up in the faultline movement and squeezed into the gap between the two moving continental fragments. It's part of the 'Highland Border Complex'; when you stand on it you are in neither the Highlands nor the Lowlands. An outcrop is 30m above the path, immediately after the crushed sandstone of the previous picture. The sunlit outcrop shown here is on the slope of Conic Hill.

OVERLEAF Inchcailloch is the island of the 'cailleach': a term translated as crone, hag, wifie or witch. This particular witch or wifie was the Irish princess St Kentigerna, mother of St Fillan whose chapel was near Tyndrum. Assuming mother and son were on visiting terms, they become the earliest named users of the West Highland Way.

Looking across to Ben Lomond from the Luss hills on the western side. The West Highland Way follows the whole of the wooded shoreline seen in this picture.

LOCH LOMOND
Milarrochy to Ardleish
18 miles/28 km

At about 7m above sea level, Lomond is Scotland's lowest loch as well as its largest. Even so, would it be so celebrated without its song? It was written by a soldier from the Rising of 1715, lying in Carlisle Castle and condemned to hang. 'I'll tak' the high road' – the quick way home was to be the flight of his spirit northwards after death.

From Balmaha, the West Highland Way continues along the loch-side into a wood. That wood takes some time to get through. It extends alongside Loch Lomond for a long day's walk of 20 miles. Variety is provided by the path itself: sometimes smooth and park-like; sometimes a fast and comfortable vehicle track; but for the 4 miles to Doune, it's a rugged reminder of the hiking conditions of 300 years ago. It's good that this short stretch does retain the au-thentic feel of the historic Highland through-routes. As a reminder, here's Walter Scott's description of this country before it was opened by roads.

'It was broken up into narrow valleys, the habitable part of which bore no proportion to the huge wilderness of forest, rocks, and precipices by which they were encircled, and which was, moreover, full of inextricable passes, morasses, and natural strengths, unknown to any but the inhabitants themselves, where a few men acquainted with the ground were capable, with ordinary address, of baffling the pursuit of numbers.'

Behind Ben Lomond the West Highland Way follows a whole lot more wooded shoreline, northwards up the loch – seen here from Cruach Tairbeirt.

41

LEFT Hitching stone at Rowardennan Hotel, where the road along Loch Lomond's eastern shore ends.

BELOW The polished granite of the war memorial at Rowardennan sits uneasily in its landscape of grey schist. The Rowardennan Estate was designated in 1997 as the Ben Lomond National Memorial Park, commemorating Scots who died in the Second World War. It thus formed the kernel of the much larger Loch Lomond and the Trossachs National Park, established five years later.

RIGHT Smoothed shoreline rocks just beyond the war memorial at Rowardennan Pier show the scratch-marks left by the glacier which carved out Loch Lomond. The last remnant of that glacier melted just 14,000 years ago. The hole gouged out by the ice is 600ft deep, and it initially filled up with sea water. The slight lifting of the land as the ice melted off it, together with silt and gravel carried by the River Endrick, has since cut the loch off at its base. During its gradual transformation to fresh water, one species of sea fish managed to evolve into Loch Lomond's unique freshwater herring, which is called the powan.

ABOVE While the path along Loch Lomond side is agreeably varied, even more variety could be provided by visiting the summit of Ben Lomond – a side trip of five or six hours from Rowardennan. This is the southernmost of Scotland's high mountains (over 3,000ft), so no other peaks extend above the cloud sea which stretches back across the Lowlands.

LEFT Loch Lomond's damp oakwoods encourage the growth of the fern called maidenhair spleenwort.

TOP LEFT Rowchoish bothy, north of Rowardennan, is the first of two simple unlocked shelters alongside Loch Lomond. Open to 'all who love wild and lonely places', bothies are maintained by volunteers of the Mountain Bothies Association. Being so close both to the busy footpath and to Glasgow, Rowchoish and Doune Byre can be low on loneliness and become, in high summer, somewhat squalid.

TOP RIGHT Inside Rowchoish bothy.

ABOVE LEFT Two miles short of Inversnaid, the West Highland Way passes Cuilness (Cailness on OS maps). The inhabitants of this well-maintained cottage must reach it by a 9-mile Landrover track which, in its final mile, descends 1,000ft (300m) to the loch side. The shepherd here in the 1930s had no such convenience: he reached the outside world by the lochside path, or by boat. As some compensation, he earned 3/6d (about £9 today) a week from the Royal Mail for acting as his own postman.

ABOVE RIGHT Flowering cherry and birch trunks at Cuilness.

ABOVE Inversnaid Hotel, seen across Loch Lomond from Inveruglas.

LEFT 'Three pyramidal mountains on the opposite side of Loch Lomond . . . which under certain accidents of weather must be very grand' – so wrote Dorothy Wordsworth in 1803. Beinn Narnain and Ben Vane, from the path south of Doune. Before the coming of the Loch Lomond glacier, the stream from this valley (Inveruglas Water) continued eastwards, 150m above the current loch and the Inversnaid Hotel, to drain into the valley of Loch Arklet and Loch Katrine.

The Arklet Falls at Inversnaid; the West
Highland Way crosses the footbridge
above. The poet-priest Gerard Manley
Hopkins stopped off here, and saw his own
ontological despair trapped in the bottom
of the waterfall.

A windpuff-bonnet of fawn-froth
Turns and twindles over the broth
Of a pool so pitchblack, fell-frowning,
It rounds and rounds Despair to drowning.

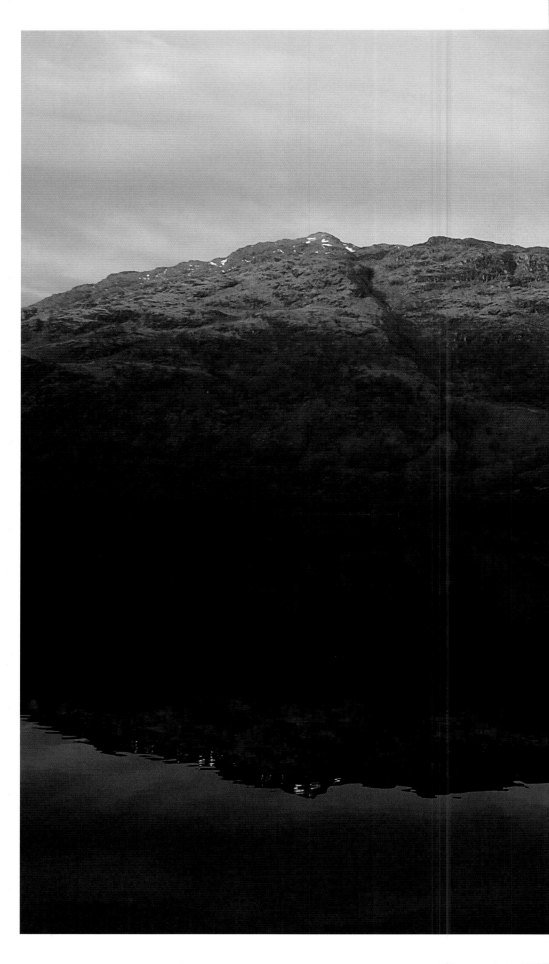

TOP Doune Byre bothy, at dawn, with Ben Lui showing above the head of Loch Lomond.

ABOVE White-walled Doune, and the unpainted Doune Byre bothy, seen across Loch Lomond.

RIGHT A dawn view across Loch Lomond to Ben Vorlich and Stuckendroin farm, from just south of the Ardleish–Ardlui ferry. It was tempting to submit this photo upside down to see if anybody noticed.

GLEN FALLOCH
Ardleish to Crianlarich
8 miles/13 km

One last look back along Loch Lomond, and then the great valley runs northwards. It will do so, with a couple of name changes, for another two days. This is a grand highway, carved by a great glacier heading south out of Rannoch Moor, used by those whooper swans aiming for Iceland, and used today by the A82, the West Highland Railway, and a couple of high-voltage power lines.

But the valley is big enough for everybody. The river Falloch, dashing white between its rocks, obliterates the sound of that busy A82 road. Alongside the path are alder trees and hazels and scattered ancient pines.

There's a fine open feel to the pathway, too, once it rises above the road and river. For the first time since Conic Hill, you look long-distance, to a single white farm house, and above it the mountains: An Caisteal and Cruach Ardrain. These are the green hills, lumps of rough country where grassland rises steeply to a skyline crinkled by a few grey rocks. At the corner above Crianlarich stands Ben More, aptly if boring named as the 'big hill', and the next of the West Highland Way's supersized waymarker signposts.

LEFT Loch Lomond head, Ardlui, and Glen Falloch from the slopes of Ben Vorlich. The lowest part of River Falloch was enlarged to a canal so that lake steamers could pass up to Inverarnan, where travellers transferred to the stagecoach. From the loch's head, the West Highland Way passes through the col behind the small hill Cnap Mor, then along the wooded slope below the white flash of Beinglas Falls. At the glen bends to the right, its track can be seen slanting up through the trees.

ABOVE Some wildlife is reasonably easy to spot. This toad was crossing the West Highland Way looking for a spawning pool in the ditches alongside.

FAR LEFT Yellow mountain saxifrage flowers in high summer on damp outcrops below Beinglas Falls.

LEFT Beinglas Falls are only seen obliquely from the small path leading up from Beinglas camp site. This autumn view is from the Inverarnan Hotel.

BELOW Beinglas Falls, looking back across River Falloch to Ben Vorlich. It's July; the birches are in luxuriant leaf and the bell heather is just starting to flower. Bell heather tends to form individual clumps, often on the better-drained rocky outcrops. Three or four weeks later, from August into September, the ling with its much smaller flowers and leaves forms a continuous purple carpet across the moorland.

Inverarnan Hotel bills itself as 'Pub of the Year 1705'. That's when it was established to cater for cattle drovers passing southwards along the line of the West Highland Way. Rob Roy himself joined the main drove road at this point, arriving through a high hill pass above Beinglas Falls.

The inn was not quite a century old when the poet Coleridge stopped off after a walk from Inveruglas along the west side of Loch Lomond, and found the service unsatisfactory. 'Waited an hour and a half for a dish of tea, the most civil promises all the while. This a fair specimen of Highland Manners.'

Probably your best chance of spotting the black bear or a golden eagle – in the bar at Inverarnan. Black bears, a trail hazard in California and the Appalachians, are not normally considered a feature of the West Highland Way.

Seen from the roadside, the inn's top right window is not a window at all. The customer can only wonder what centuries-old scandal is walled up in this attic. The hotel admits to six separate hauntings. There's a murdered drover who screams through the night corridors. There's old George, who hasn't abandoned his favourite bar stool simply because of being dead. But the worst one is the young girl drowned in River Falloch 200 years ago. She was laid out in the inn, and visitors sometimes wake to find her cold and wet beside them in the bed.

ABOVE View north up Glen Falloch. 'Pursued my way up Glen Falloch toward Tyndrum, the glen narrowing, the river becoming more and more wild and rocky, running and roaming among alders and coppice woods, the hills landlocking the glen with less than half a mile interspace, the hills not very high, but much broken, and their wildness a ragged wildness.' This is Coleridge again in 1803. He was a sick man, using the long-distance walk to break his opium addiction. Also, his shoes were falling apart after overzealous drying out at Inversnaid. Accordingly, his daily distances were very moderate: he would take three full days from Inverarnan to Fort William – admittedly by a somewhat longer route than the West Highland Way, via Ballachulish.

Most walkers today, given our better footwear, more-or-less waterproof clothing, and the greatly improved path, don't need Coleridge's three days for this stretch. We need between three-and-a-half and six days.

RIGHT The path passes above the Falls of Falloch, but it is right beside this small cataract. The river noise and its alder trees effectively cover the busy main road on the other side – at the road's present size, at least. The Lomond Trossach Tourist Board, along with Fort William Chamber of Commerce, is campaigning for a dual carriageway right through to Fort William.

Falls of Falloch: Coleridge again: 'I went with him into a field to my right, and visited a noble waterfall – during rain it must be a most noble one. The trees are old, and army, one on each side. It is one great apron with an oval pool at the bottom, but above it you look up through a rocky stream with trees and bushes, and the fall itself is marked by two great cauldrons delved out in the black rock, down which it falls – into which cauldron it boils and rebounds. This is on the river of Glenfalloch, which words signifies the Hidden Glen. I talked much with the Scotchman – the oppressions of the landlord – and he used these beautiful words: "It kills one's affection for one's country, the hardships of life, coming by change, and wi' injustice."' I would happily let Coleridge write all my captions; nobody since has done it so well. 'Army' I take to mean 'with lots of arms on'. The shepherd refers to the Highland Clearances, the forcible removal of the glen's people to clear the land for sheep.

LEFT Power lines accompany the path along Glen Falloch. This intrepid repairman could well be descended from cattle thieves and drovers.

BELOW 'I had been lost in reverie and on awaking found . . . high, separating mountains, pyramids, cones, ridges, which one might stride across, some running straight on, some curving into arcs of circles, and forming basons and hollows. A break of an inverted triangle shape, and a naked sugar loaf looks in from a distant country. A vast multitude of sheep, alas! the very first time I ever looked at sheep with melancholy and indignant feelings!'

Coleridge looks across Glen Falloch at the Crianlarich Munros – here, Cruach Ardrain, with some regenerating pine and birch wood in the foreground. The 'sugar loaf' is possibly Ben More. The indignation was because of the Clearances, mentioned above.

RIGHT Schist isn't all the same. Where the underground cooking and crushing has been slightly less forcible, different minerals make the silvery, glistening variant called phyllite.

FAR RIGHT Where the heat and pressure have increased beyond a certain point, corresponding with about 20 miles underground, the semi-precious garnets form within the schist. They are seen in the path on the final part of this section, starting from the track junction a mile before Keilator, and continuing through the plantations above Crianlarich. The ones in this path stone are about 5mm across.

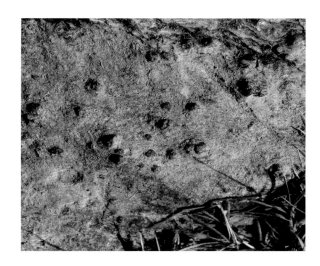

BELOW Ben More stands above the corner where Glen Falloch becomes Strath Fillan. At 1,174m or 3,852ft high, it offers to hillwalkers the longest slope of steep grass in Scotland.

STRATH FILLAN
Crianlarich to Bridge of Orchy
12½ miles/21 km

The wood pulp plantations above Crianlarich are grim when you're in them and ugly from outside. The West Highland Way hurries through, then dashes across the A82 to make the acquaintance of River Fillan. It's a new river, but the same alders and sparkling water – and the same long valley, a huge 'U' through the hills, heading ever northwards towards Rannoch.

This part of the path is haunted by two long-distance men of long ago. Back in the ninth century, St Fillan strode across Scotland and back again before making his base here, above a river pool whose healing powers are only slightly effective against blisters. Seven centuries later, the extended hikes of Robert the Bruce were interrupted by the occasional swordfight.

Emerging from Tyndrum, you're impressed by the high cone of Beinn Odhar – at least until you come around its flank, to be confronted by impossibly pointed Beinn Dorain, sung about in 554 lines of Gaelic verse by Duncan Ban. The way passes below their tall shapely slopes, cut by stream runnels like folded curtains. Picked up by a low sun, that hillside texture in summer green, or autumn brown, has a pleasant simplicity, and is even better in winter white.

ABOVE Partly obscured, Glen Falloch and the West Highland Way run in from the left of this photo taken from Cruach Ardrain. Having turned the corner at Crianlarich (bottom right), the West Highland Way heads north up Strath Fillan before bending slightly right at Tyndrum. Directly above the right-hand edge of Crianlarich, half-hidden behind Ben Challum, is Ben Nevis. The nearer mountain to left is Ben Lui.

LEFT Above Crianlarich, a narrow gap-line marks the West Highland Way passing through the forestry plantations. In this 'boots-eye view' from the summit of Ben More, Ben Lui and distant Ben Cruachan form a backdrop. Views from the path itself are mostly of spruce twigs.

BELOW Woolly hair moss matches the schist rocks on which it grows.

ABOVE River Fillan from the bridge at Kirkton, looking downstream to Cruach Ardrain.

RIGHT The bridge at Kirkton.

Strath Fillan runs directly away from Ben More, which as you walk north does gradually loom less large. It's seen here, with its twin peak Stob Binnein behind, from the track to Kirkton.

ABOVE, FAR LEFT St Fillan's Priory at Kirkton. Son of an Irish chieftain and Saint Kentigerna, the missionary and hermit Fillan criss-crossed Scotland from Perthshire to Pittenweem before settling in Strath Fillan. He died in about AD 777.

During the building of his priory, a wolf killed one of the oxen hauling in stones. Fillan gave the beast a telling-off; and the remorseful wolf took over the cart-hauling duties of its recent lunch. Fillan's name means 'little wolf'.

It's said that the saint's left arm was phosphorescent, like a very large glow-worm: this he found useful for reading and writing the Scriptures after dark. The Bernane, his brass bell, would fly through the air when he called it. A surprised visitor shot an arrow at the flying bell and cracked it. It is now kept at the Museum of Scotland in Edinburgh.

ABOVE, MIDDLE Graveyard at Kirkton, with Beinn Odhar. Fillan's original chapel was at his healing pool, just upstream. Robert the Bruce rebuilt and re-endowed the Augustinian priory in gratitude for favours bestowed by the saint at Bannockburn. Bruce had summoned the reliquary with Fillan's arm (the fillet of Fillan, one could say) to be carried in front of his army. Its hereditary keeper or 'Dewar' apparently didn't trust the battle-winning qualities of his own relic. Not wanting to lose it to the English, he kept it safely at home, bringing only the empty reliquary. But during the preliminary prayers before the battle, the case flew open, with the self-illumining arm having miraculously teleported back into its place. Bruce went on to win the battle against King Edward.

ABOVE RIGHT Waterfall just above Auchtertyre farm.

LEFT BELOW Thomas Pennant, in 1772 the first travel writer up the West Highland Way, describes St Fillan's healing pool. 'He is pleased to take under his protection the disordered in mind; and works wonderful cures, say his votaries, even to this day. The unhappy lunatics are brought here by their friends, who first perform the ceremony of the Deasil [walking clockwise, as the sun] thrice round a neighbouring cairn; afterwards offer on it their rags, or a little bunch of heath tied with worsted; then thrice immerge the patient in a holy pool of the river, and, to conclude, leave him fast bound the whole night in the neighbouring chapel. But it often happens that death proves the angel that releases the afflicted, before the morrow, from all the troubles of this life.'

At Tyndrum Rob Roy caught up with a land agent of the Earl of Breadalbane who had been evicting Macgregors. The conversation may have gone something like this:

Rob Roy: 'Don't you know these people are under my protection?'
Land Agent (signing the papers to restore the house to its owners): 'Rob, I don't know what I was thinking of. I must have been crazy.'
Rob Roy: 'Well you're in luck, then. You've come to exactly the right place.'

And then the unfortunate land agent was stripped, ducked in the pool, and subjected to the overnight in the chapel under St Fillan's bell. It worked: by morning he was cured of any tendency to harass Clan Gregor in Strath Fillan.

RIGHT Dalrigh is 'Field of the King'. The name commemorates a small skirmish of Robert the Bruce in the summer of 1306.

After his makeshift coronation at Scone he was defeated by pro-English forces at Methven. Having escaped the battlefield, he met the enemy again at Loch Tay and was defeated again. Over the next few months, he suffered further defeats in almost every corner of Scotland, from Glen Tilt to Galloway. He was fleeing towards the Hebrides when his trail was picked up by MacDougall of Lorn. To stop it slowing him down, Bruce disposed of his heavy broadsword in a lochan, possibly this one. The MacDougalls caught him anyway, ten minutes down the trail, alongside the River Fillan. The skirmish is recorded by historians as another defeat for the Bruce: but more importantly, it was yet another escape. A few days later he was pursued across Loch Lomond by an armed war galley, before finally getting away to Bute and then Rathlin Island.

BELOW Memorial stone at the lochan. The Scots *claidheamh mór* (claymore) weighed 6lb (2.5kg) and was four to five feet (1.5m) long. It was wielded two-handed.

OPPOSITE Beinn Odhar (dun-coloured hill) is seen from the path behind Tyndrum.

LEFT Just south of Tyndrum, the West Highland Way crosses ground poisoned by the former lead smelter.

BELOW The stream in the picture opposite drains the spoil heaps of the lead mines on Sron nan Colan; so its bed is a likely place to find minerals such as this grey galena with traces of golden pyrites or 'fool's gold'. Real gold is also found in streams hereabouts.

'Dined at Tyndrum and walked a brisk pace under the inspiration of a bottle of Burton ale, from Tyndrum to Inverooran. A fine road through a perfectly houseless moorland, the mountains on either side, behind, before, most noble – though green. I seemed to think that these high green mountains, so furrowed, delved, and wrinkled with torrents, are still wilder than craggy mountains. The mountains were all detached, a great beauty!' Caption again by Coleridge (1803). The detached hills are Beinn Dorain (left) and Beinn a' Chaisteil. The West Highland Way runs along the base of the two hills.

Pennant adds a traditional weather forecasting technique: 'In my passage, in 1769, from the King's-house to this place [Tyndrum], I rode near the mountains of Bendoran. One of them is celebrated for the hollow sound it sends forth about twenty-four hours before any heavy rain. The spirit of the mountain shrieks; warns the peasants to shelter their flocks.'

ABOVE Around the base of Beinn Dorain, the West Highland Railway takes a huge horseshoe into the Auch Gleann, crossing two viaducts. The direct route would have required a single, much longer and more expensive viaduct. However, these and other sharp bends limit the trains to a speed of 30mph.

For its wild crossing of Rannoch Moor, the railway was floated on bundles of brushwood sunk into the bog. Supposedly, the weight of the train sinks the line by a couple of feet, meaning that the engine must haul uphill in both directions.

Pictured here is the Auch Gleann viaduct, also glimpsed in the previous picture. The West Highland Way short-cuts across the loop.

BELOW Beinn Dorain rises above Ais an t-Sidhean. The stonework up to door-top level is from Duncan Ban's time.

Ais an t-Sidhean is three miles up Auch Gleann on a side-track. Duncan Ban MacIntyre, who served here as gamekeeper to the Earl of Breadalbane, wrote 554 lines of Gaelic verse in praise of Beinn Dorain. He was born in 1724, and was in a sense the first West Highland Way ranger, as he also served at Inveroran and in Glen Etive under Buachaille Etive Mor. Most of his poem is in praise of Dorain's deer, and the thrill of killing them. His favourite gun was called Nic Coiseim (1746–66). The lines on Coire Frithe can be enjoyed even without any Gaelic:

Gu stobanach stacanach
Slocanach laganach
Cnocanach cnapanach
Caiteanach ròmach,
Pasganach badanach
Bachlagach bòidheach

Stob, stac, sloc, lagan, cnoc and cnap may be familiar to students of Gaelic hill naming as a pointy hill, a stack-shaped hill, a slot-pass, a hollow, and two sorts of hillock. A translation as rough as Dorain's own slopes might run:

So peaky and spiky
So slotted and hollow-ish
Humpy and hummocky
Craggy and shaggy
Tufted and tussocky
Clumpy and lovely.

OVERLEAF River Orchy above Bridge of Orchy, looking south.

71

RANNOCH MOOR
Bridge of Orchy to Kings House
12½ miles/20 km

Loch Tulla, looking across to the levels around Inveroran Hotel. These meadows were a traditional 'stance' or overnight grazing ground for the droves on their way southwards: it must have been a welcome haven after the crossing of Rannoch Moor. The Inveroran Hotel owes its existence to this droving traffic: indeed, the traditional right of wild camping at the roadside west of the hotel may be continuous back to droving times. Above, Ben Starav stands above the furthest end of Gleann Shira.

Bridge of Orchy is where the path turns aside, at last, from the A82, and strikes its own way – except that its own way is actually the old way. The military road crosses the hill shoulder to Loch Tulla, and then Thomas Telford's well-founded stony way passes under the high Black Mount, around the edge of Rannoch Moor.

Here is Britain's biggest and bleakest piece of peat. Its 20 miles of heather and water are criss-crossed with the forgotten routes of marauding Campbells and MacDonalds, and of the later cattle drovers. Today these bleak acres are the domain of the red deer, disturbed only by the thrice-daily trains to Fort William and the distant murmur of the A82.

The twigs of the heather are touched with gold as the sun rises across the moorland. But when low cloud blows across the moorland, it's simply bleak. After 7 miles you come to a ruin, and a small stone bridge built by Thomas Telford. Four more miles, and there's the monument to a deceased deer-stalker. There's a single blue lochan, and on the left the high yellow grass and black crag of Coire Ba, the hollow of the red deer.

ABOVE Doire Darach, a remnant of ancient pine forest above Loch Tulla. Scots pine once covered the greater part of Highland Scotland apart from the highest mountains which were bare stones, and the warmer glens and western coasts where oaks grew instead. Over centuries the trees were cleared for pastureland, or burnt to flush out outlaws and bandits. Later they were felled for shipbuilding, for charcoal to fuel iron smelters, and to make way for sheep. Red deer encouraged by estate owners of the nineteenth century nibbled away any regrowing saplings. Today, temporary fencing against deer is allowing the gradual recovery of scattered fragments such as this one, seen below the West Highland Way.

After rounding the head of the loch, the West Highland Way will continue across the moorland opposite.

RIGHT On an island in one of Rannoch Moor's many lochs, pine and larch show how they can grow where deer do not destroy the young trees.

LEFT This cairn stands at the high point of the West Highland Way as it crosses from Bridge of Orchy to Loch Tulla. This view looks back to Beinn an Dothaidh and Beinn Dorain, which stand directly above Bridge of Orchy.

BELOW LEFT A herd of hinds – female red deer – crosses the West Highland Way opposite Inveroran Hotel. This photo was taken at dusk in early April. In high summer, the deer head further uphill to enjoy the fresh growth and escape the midges.

BELOW RIGHT The sturdy stonework here may be original, from the 1820s, although Telford covered it with a layer of fine gravel for the hooves of the cattle. Six miles away southwards, at the other edge of the moor, the hills are Beinn Achaladair and (looking like a single hill) Beinn an Dothaidh with Beinn Dorain.

LEFT 'Eighteen miles of beautiful road, such as you may see in noblemen's pleasure grounds, through a wide wide moor, with rocky rivers, mountains of all shapes, scarr'd and lay'd open, but none craggy. The rain all the way, except now and then a blow off that discovered all the forms of the mountains and that I had lost nothing else. Add to these large moorland pools with bushy islets – and one goat – and you have the whole I saw.' So wrote Coleridge of his crossing of Rannoch Moor in 1803. The same description applies to the replacement road, built by Thomas Telford twenty years later. It's seen running across the middle of this picture just beyond the two lochans.

RIGHT A boulder of Rannoch granite on Meall Beag.

RIGHT BELOW A clean pebble of granite picked up from the path near Ba Bridge.

TOP Looking east across the moor from Ba Bridge, the half-way point in the crossing of Rannoch Moor. The nearby hill is Meall Beag, the 'small hump'.

ABOVE Walkers rest on Ba Bridge.

ABOVE Across Rannoch Moor, from the memorial to one Ronald Harvey which stands on Meall Mor.

RIGHT This unmarked cairn stands above the high point of the West Highland Way before it descends towards Kings House. It is a memorial to Colonel Peter Fleming, the older brother of the James Bond creator Ian Fleming. Peter was an adventurer in his own right and a noted travel writer. He suffered a heart attack here while stalking deer in 1971. The Fleming family still owns the Blackmount Estate.

ABOVE The ruined Ba Cottage.

LEFT This well-weathered sign, possibly as old as the West Highland Way itself, stands where the old road crosses the new one (A82) below the White Corries ski area.

RIGHT Looking across one of Rannoch Moor's many lochs to the Black Mount.

THE DEVIL'S STAIRCASE
Kings House to Kinlochleven
8 miles/13 km

After the bleakness of Rannoch, the crossing of the Devil's Staircase sees the West Highland Way surrounded by mountains. And what mountains! Behind are the hills of Etive: the steep northern end of the Black Mount, and the magnificent cone of Buachaille Etive Mor. To the west is a glimpse into the shaded hollow of Glen Coe and the grim triple pillars of Bidean nam Bian.

You reach the top of the path so carefully zig-zagged by Major Caulfeild's miserable redcoats, who were paid an inadequate sixpence per day extra in compensation for the midge bites. And suddenly, a whole new mountain mass lies in front. The swinging ridgeline of the Mamores will hang over the path from here to Kinlochleven, and onwards into the final day of the walk. Above and behind is the great hunched shape of Ben Nevis.

Having gained 1,000ft of altitude northwards from Loch Lomond, and another 1,000ft in the last mile up the Devil's Staircase, the way now loses all of that in the descent to Kinlochleven. Heather and rock, mountains all around, and the deep glen of River Leven all oak trees, with the sound of waterfalls drifting up the surrounding slopes: here is no work of man apart from the path that brought you. Well, there is also the huge six-fold metal pipeline down to the turbines at Kinlochmore . . .

A deep-water loch, along with steep mountains and plenty of rain for electric generation, brought the aluminium factory; and the aluminium factory brought the village of Kinlochleven. And (for those peeved at the pipeline) without Kinlochleven, where would be the night's bar meal and cosy bunkhouse?

The West Highland Way on
the old military road one
mile west of Kings House.

Modern path builders
have hit on the same
cobbled paving for fords as
Major Caulfeild's redcoats
used for the building
of the original military
road. This neat piece of
construction is near the
top of the descent towards
Kinlochleven.

The Mamores are seen
on the descent from the
Devil's Staircase pass.

LEFT The West Highland Way descends from the left of the picture to the top of the Kinlochleven hydro pipeline. The waterfalls seen here are on-off ones, depending on whether any spare water is arriving along the aqueduct from Blackwater Reservoir. The ridge line above is the Aonach Eagach, a famous mountain scramble which on its other side overlooks Glen Coe.

BELOW, LEFT AND RIGHT The hydro pipeline down to Kinlochleven.

ABOVE From Altnafeadh onwards, pinkish volcanic rhyolite is seen among the path stones. This lump (top) shows the shape of a cooling lava flow of 400 million years ago. Less common in the path is the darker-coloured andesite (bottom). These two pebbles are probably from an intrusive dyke or sill, and contain crystals of white feldspar. Above the larger black pebble is a similarly crystalline pink rhyolite. The surrounding stones are Rannoch granite, with one pale lump of quartzite.

RIGHT As the West Highland Way's track approaches the bridge at the edge of Kinlochleven it crosses a wide dyke of the reddish rhyolite. From the bridge itself, the rhyolite dyke can be seen crossing the River Leven.

LAIRIG MOR
Kinlochleven to Nevis Forest
9 miles/14 km

Four miles into the Lairig Mor, as the track begins its descent after the ruined Tigh-na-sleubhaich, there stands a wobbly right-of-way signpost pointing off to the left. That route runs down to what seems to be a completely pointless point on the B863 – there isn't even a car park.

In fact it's a part of Scotland's sometime 'motorway network', from a time when a small boat across Loch Leven made far more sense than a diversion through the hills on foot or horseback. This path, in combination with the West Highland Way track, was the route south of MacIain of Glencoe in the last days of 1691. He arrived at Fort William to sign the oath of allegiance with two days to spare, only to be pointed south to Inveraray where he should have signed it. Fifty miles and two loch crossings should have been possible by the deadline, but the elderly chieftain was detained by enemies at Ballachulish. His late arrival at Inveraray was the pretext for the massacre of Glencoe two months later.

The cattle drovers too used this road, swimming their herds across the narrows of Loch Leven. It was Major Caulfeild who chose the alternative approach from Kinlochleven, accepting the high crossing of the Devil's Staircase so as to be independent of local boatmen. By 1800, wheeled traffic was using instead the longer coast road alongside Loch Linnhe. The Lairig was still busy, in summer at least, as whole villages moved uphill to its sheltered grazings. With the depopulation of the glens the glen finally fell silent – until, two centuries later, the West Highland Way brings new foot traffic along its ancient ways.

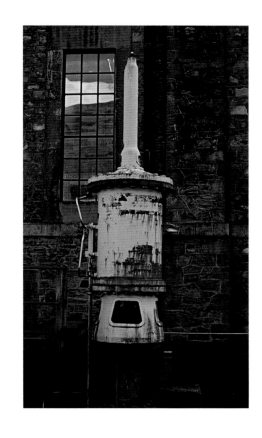

LEFT The industrial village of Kinlochleven was built around the former aluminium factory (at the near edge of the village).

ABOVE RIGHT The factory is now closed. Its hydroelectric turbines still supply power to the national grid, and its buildings house a small brewery and Britain's largest (indeed, only) artificial ice-climbing wall.

RIGHT The tailrace from the hydroelectric turbines.

Dawn view of Loch Leven
from high above the village.
At top left is the Pap of
Glencoe; at bottom right,
Mamore Lodge Hotel.

LEFT AND ABOVE Grey Mare's Tail waterfall at the edge of Kinlochleven. Visiting it is a ten-minute diversion off the West Highland Way.

Loch Leven from above the
Grey Mare's Tail waterfall.

TOP Looking down from the
Mamores ridge to Lairig
Mor and the long stony
track of the West Highland
Way.

ABOVE The same view, but
backwards: from Lairig
Mor, up towards Stob Ban.

RIGHT The West Highland Way leaves Kinlochleven.

BELOW The ruined Tigh-na-sleubhaich stands near the high point of the Lairig Mor. The valley appears to end ahead, but in fact bends downhill and to the right.

GLEN NEVIS
Nevis Forest to Fort William
6 miles/10 km

The poet Coleridge came into Glen Nevis in 1803, and was disappointed, finding it a 'poor copy' of Keswick's River Greta. But ten minutes later, the river improved most surprisingly, and by the Polldubh Falls he lapsed into near-incoherence: 'The ledge-precipicy side of the proboscis of an elephant, with savage trees, all straight, and by that extreme straightness harmonizing with the perpendicularity of the little precipices, of which the great precipice is made up.' The West Highland Way, regrettably, visits only the lower end of the glen. Glen Nevis is indeed one of Scotland's finest: but not around Achintee. Since 1803, it's been further defaced with forestry plantations, car parks and caravan sites.

Today, beauty is no longer all around us, but something we need to seek out. Those not focused on the final 2 miles of tarmac can find it by crossing the footbridge at the visitor centre, and entering Fort William along the riverbank. Better still, turn not down the glen but up it (there's a convenient bus service) for the Nevis gorge, and the extraordinary waterfall at Steall. Meanwhile, something far beyond mere prettiness is found on the mountaineers' way up big Ben Nevis: not by its heavily used Mountain Trail from Achintee, but the intimidating northern face and the fine rock ridge from Carn Mor Dearg.

But for the final mile of the West Highland Way, lower Glen Nevis teaches that the countryside can't be taken for granted. Today's world seems, indeed, in a tremendous hurry to wreck it. But those arriving on foot after 95 miles of Loch Lomond, Rannoch, and Glen Coe know that, above the caravan site and the spruce trees, the Highlands are still a fine, fine place.

Ben Nevis from Dun Deardail, where the West Highland Way turns down into Glen Nevis.

LEFT A few steps off the West Highland Way is the old Glen Nevis burial ground. It is found through a wooden gateway on the left, 50m before the path reaches the tarmac of the Glen Nevis road. Though not much more than 200 years old, the stones have built up an impressive patina of mosses and lichen in the green gloom below beech trees.

ABOVE Seen from its glen, Ben Nevis appears as a big – very big – slope of stones. Its more interesting face overlooks its great northern corrie in two miles of continuous crag. The footbridge opposite Glen Nevis Youth Hostel is one start-point for the mountain's arduous but busy Mountain Trail.

ABOVE The Roaring Mill (Eas a' Chlaiginn) in River Nevis is glimpsed through roadside trees from the West Highland Way, but better seen by those who choose the riverside path into Fort William.

RIGHT Granite boulder at Roaring Mill. As it lies on sedimentary flagstones, it was presumably placed here by the Glen Nevis glacier – or else by the mythical Fingalians, amused by the grumpy face it displays. Less than a mile from the journey's end, West Highland Way walkers may be somewhat more cheerful.

TOP The Glen Nevis road carries the last mile of the West Highland Way.

ABOVE Fort William's fish restaurant stands on the jetty also used by a small passenger ferry across Loch Linnhe to Camusnagaul. Those with spare energy can use the ferry for onward walks to Glenfinnan and the wild western seaboard. Others might prefer a seal-watching boat trip, or indeed the excellent restaurant.

RIGHT End of Way marker at Glen Nevis bridge. But there are plans to add an extra kilometre into Fort William so as to connect with the start of the Great Glen Way.

OVERLEAF Ben Nevis, with Glen Nevis to its right, seen across Loch Linnhe.

THE END OF THE WAY

Looking back from the end of this book, I'm struck by how few pictures I've taken of buildings. Never was I tempted to drive through the night to catch low morning sun on the cottages of Crianlarich and Kinlochleven. When it comes to Crianlarich, low morning sun just doesn't do it. Fort William, the walk's great destination, is not the ugliest of Highland towns – that distinction goes to Aviemore. Fort William is merely the second ugliest. In the 95 miles of the way, I found one noble building: the schisty stonework of the Inverarnan Inn.

Add to that the barely legal hand-built shacks at Carbeth, plus the bridges of General Caulfeild, Thomas Telford, and the West Highland Railway. The aluminium factory at Kinlochleven has a certain grandeur. But that's it. The good bits of the Way are those points where you see no sign of man at all, apart from the footpath you stand on. The 20-mile oak wood at the back of Loch Lomond. Rannoch Moor. The descent behind the Devil's Staircase.

The mountains themselves are like the MacDonalds and Macgregors of three centuries ago – a valiant anachronism, surviving into a world where they no longer belong. To a soundtrack of lorries and motorbikes we behold Ben Lomond. Between the wires of the hydroelectric scheme we see Glen Falloch. Ben More rises majestic out of a plantation of wood-pulp.

My researches for this book took me to Tyndrum Information Centre in the rain, where an information officer was trying to find some fun for a couple of Dutch visitors. Did the visitors enjoy walking? Not especially. What they enjoyed was driving around in their car and seeing the scenery. The information centre was scented with aromatherapeutic heather preparations. A soundtrack of souped-down Scottish song drowned out the raindrops pattering on the window panes; the tourist literature wilted in the soggy air. She gave the Dutch people a timetable for the gondola at Aonach Mor. Lochaber, on a rainy day in May – maybe. For who wants to spend time in Tyndrum?

Mentioned earlier in the book were three plagues of old Argyll: the bracken, the midges, and the Campbells. Bracken results from overgrazing, and sheep stocks are being somewhat reduced. The Campbells are, these days, pretty much a spent force. Midges, of course, are still with us. But the first plague of today is the spruce tree. The simple

The West Highland Way below An Caisteal. Along Glen Falloch there will always be a glimpse of a power pylon. The A82 crosses the path a mile south of this point. Here it is out of sight in the hollow below the foreground pastures.

slopes of Strath Fillan were designated by Nature as oakwoods and pine, with birches above. They were turned by the sheep into damp grassland, folded with linear streams like hanging curtains.

That is replaced today with dark plantations in featureless green. Spruce forest in a semi-wild state, as around the High Tatras of Slovakia, has a gloom that can get to you: the drooping branches with their grey lichen, the sunbeams falling into soggy moss. But the wood pulp plantations of Drymen or Crianlarich are grim when you're in them and ugly from outside.

The second curse of Crianlarich is the A82 road. From Loch Lomond to Loch Tulla, the poor old West Highland Way is hardly out of earshot of its rumble, and often close enough to catch the evocative swish of wheels in rainwater. In a blind test, those who expressed a preference slightly preferred a distant motorway to the sound of waterfalls. But however much we may enjoy the traffic murmur, the A82's ever-moving line of boxy lorries and white vans effectively wrecks any wilderness feel. The U-shaped Fillan and Falloch glens waft the engine noises up the surrounding slopes to the summit plateau.

The Fort William Chamber of Commerce, as well as the Lomond-Trossach Etc Tourist Board, want this road upgraded to dual carriageway all the way. Well, the western shore of Loch Lomond is already wrecked, we shouldn't worry about making that a bit worse. Glen Falloch and Strath Fillan: road widening would make it even harder for the tourist lady at Tyndrum to pretend that it's a pretty place. Rannoch Moor is big enough to take an extra carriageway. But Glen Coe, the 'Glen of Weeping' – is its real value as a racketing highway for the busy

businessman and the tourist eager for the rain-sodden malls of Fort William?

A moment of silent contemplation, then, for the days when the West Highland Way was a through route for reivers, drovers and Dorothy Wordsworth, rather than a roadside pavement: when the valleys were bright birch, and the sound of a waterfall on the opposing slope. Must we drive at 70mph along Loch Lomond in search of the 'unspoilt' wilderness somewhere further on? Each decade brings new ugliness, with pylons, and breezeblock buildings, and bulldozed Landrover tracks, and noise. Each year we travel slightly faster, to somewhere slightly less worth travelling to.

For it's not the mountains that are out of adjustment, trying to lead an inappropriate cattle-thieving lifestyle in a world where it simply doesn't work. And it's not the midge that's the main curse of Perthshire. When Rob Roy chased cows across the Trossachs, he was one of 700 million human beings. Today we are ten times that number, and doubling every 50 years. In a couple of centuries we have burnt the oil that took hundreds of millions of years to form, as well as destroying most of the world's woods, and unbalancing (perhaps not yet permanently) the atmosphere and climate. The hills will endure. Can we say as much for ourselves?

And the Highlanders, the clansmen and women of 200 years ago. They were at home in this land as we in our Chinese-made boots and synthetic waterproofs will never be. A brave, loyal, adventurous people, whose tragedy it was to confront impossible changes in the world around them. Their lifestyle may, within our lifetimes, come to have

LEFT Loch Lomond, and the pylons of the Sloy hydroelectric scheme. When pylons started to stride across the landscape, 70 years ago, some saw them as majestic symbols of the brave new technological world. Lochs Lomond and Tulla are unusual in the Highlands in not having been dammed to provide electricity.

At Altnafeadh the West Highland Way bids farewell to the A82, faithful companion for almost 50 miles. No more the swish of wheels in rainwater, the procession of lorries through every view, the snarl of the early morning motorbike. In the event, Caulfeild's old road has usually run a little way up the valley side, for drier going and smaller stream culverts, and its modern neighbour has been rather less intrusive than a study of the map would suggest. I doubt if we'll say the same, if it happens, of the dual-carriageway enlargement currently promoted by Highland Council which already refers to Falloch and Fillan as the 'A82 Corridor'.

an unexpected relevance, as we learn (those of us who survive) to live in a world without cars and computers, without hospitals and police and central government: a world with far fewer folk in it, in small groups of family and tribe; a world where hungry neighbours come over the hill and steal your cattle; where your life depends on your local warlord and how clever he is at setting ambushes along the loch side; where a nice night in means a smoky hut and a bard rambling on about the last clan chief but three.

Walking the 95 miles, then, should make us ashamed of our own ugliness. But it will make us aware, also, of the beauty of our world: the green light under the summer oaks; the autumn bellowing of the stags; the chill of dawn as the mists rise out of Rannoch Moor; the scent of sun-warmed heather on Cnap Mor, and the view all along the water, as winter turns to spring and the swans fly north up Loch Lomond.

Walker on Loch Lomond side south of Inversnaid.

Rannoch Moor, to Beinn Achaladair.

FURTHER READING AND BIBLIOGRAPHY

Guidebooks and Maps for the West Highland Way

The route is clear and well waymarked. I did not carry a guidebook, and only referred to a map (the Harvey strip map) once or twice a day.

West Highland Way by Roger Smith (Mercat Press, 9th Edition 2010; or the original edition *West Highland Way Official Guide* by Robert Aitken (HMSO, 1980). Of many guidebooks, this one has, to my mind, the most interesting background information.

The West Highland Way (2008 edition) by Jacquetta Megarry (Rucksack Readers). Spiral bound and waterproof, this is probably the most compact and practical for actual route guidance, and includes a map at 1:100,000 scale.

West Highland Way Footprint Map/Guide (Stirling Surveys). The simplest and cheapest, and quite adequate.

West Highland Way Route Map (Harvey). This map is at 1:40,000 with detailed contours and is printed on robust polythene. It offers a strip several kilometres wide, which means that it is also good for ascending nearby peaks, including Ben Lomond and Ben Nevis.

Background reading (plus one film)

Rob Roy Macgregor: his Life and Times by W.H. Murray (paperback, Canongate). A well-researched and lively biography, somewhat biased in favour of the Highlanders (apart from the Campbells) and none the worse for that.

Rob Roy directed by Michael Caton-Jones (1995). Starring Liam Neeson and Jessica Lange, the film is derived from Murray's biography. There's some sound history but also various romantic departures.

Rob Roy by Sir Walter Scott (1817, several paperback editions in print). Rob is not the principal character and only appears half way through. As Waverley novels go this is a fairly readable one, and also fairly short. Get an edition that includes the extended historical introduction: Scott talked to people who in youth actually knew Rob Roy.

Glencoe: The Story of the Massacre by John Prebble (paperback, Penguin, 1968). Like Bill Murray, John Prebble is both scholarly and passionate. The real story of the Glencoe Massacre is more complicated, but just as sad, as the over-simplified legend. Both Murray and Prebble go beyond their immediate subjects to give an overview of the life of the clans.

Recollections of a Tour Made in Scotland by Dorothy Wordsworth (included in *Dorothy Wordsworth: A Longman Cultural Edition* edited by Susan Levin). Written for publication, so not quite so lively as her Grasmere Journal, but Dorothy has an observant eye and a gift for making friends. 'To a Highland Girl, at Inversneyde', written by William on the journey, is also included. The Wordsworths travelled up the west side of Loch Lomond, then after a diversion to the west coast and Glen Coe came down the West Highland Way southwards from Kings House to Crianlarich.

Coleridge among the Lakes and Mountains (Folio Society, 1991, out of print, but cheaply available second-hand). Selections from his notebooks and letters covering the Somerset and Lake District years as well as the tour of 1803, with many contemporary illustrations. Accompanying the Wordsworths up Loch Lomond, he continued northwards on foot along the West Highland Way to Kings House, then to Fort William by Glen Coe and Loch Linnhe.

Hostile Habitats: Scotland's Mountain Environment (SMT with Scottish Natural Heritage). A hillwalker's guide to geology, landforms, vegetation and wildlife.

Scottish Outdoor Access Code (Scottish Natural Heritage). Since 2005, walkers and campers have unrestricted access to virtually all land in Scotland, provided that access is taken 'responsibly'. The rights and responsibilities of walkers and of land managers are outlined in the Access Code. It is available free, or as a download from the SNH website.